# About Marsupials

# About Marsupials

## A Guide for Children

Cathryn Sill

*Illustrated by John Sill*

Ω

PEACHTREE

ATLANTA

For the One who created marsupials.

—*Genesis* 1:25

Published by
PEACHTREE PUBLISHERS
1700 Chattahoochee Avenue
Atlanta, Georgia 30318-2112
*www.peachtree-online.com*

Illustrations created in watercolor on archival quality 100% rag watercolor paper
Text and titles set in Novarese from Adobe Systems

Printed in October 2013 by Imago in Singapore
10 9 8 7 6 5 4 3 (hardcover)
10 9 8 7 6 5 4 3 (trade paperback)

**Library of Congress Cataloging-in-Publication Data**

Sill, Cathryn P., 1953-
    About marsupials : a guide for children / Cathryn Sill ; illustrated by John Sill.
       p. cm
    ISBN 13: 978-1-56145-358-0 / ISBN 10: 1-56145-358-7 (hardcover)
    ISBN 13: 978-1-56145-407-5 / ISBN 10: 1-56145-407-9 (trade paperback)
1.. Marsupials--Juvenile literature.  I. Sill, John, ill. II. Title.
QL737.M3S55 2006
599.2--dc22
              2005020582

# About Marsupials

Marsupials are mammals whose babies are born tiny and helpless.

Most mother marsupials have a pouch on their bellies to keep the babies safe as they drink milk and grow.

2

Some marsupials do not have a pouch.

3

Marsupials move by jumping, climbing, gliding, or running.

4

They may live in trees...

PLATE 6
*Grizzled Tree Kangaroo*

on the ground...

PLATE 7
*Greater Bilby*

6

or underground.

PLATE 8
*Marsupial Mole*

One kind of marsupial lives in water part of the time.

8

Many marsupials are nocturnal—they hunt and eat at night.

9

Others look for food during the day.

16

Some marsupials eat meat.

PLATE 12
*Tasmanian Devil*

Some eat plants.

12

A few eat both meat and plants.

13

Marsupials may be as big as a man…

14

or as small as a mouse.

PLATE 16
*Fat-tailed Dunnart*

15

It is important to protect marsupials and
the places where they live.

16

# Afterword

**PLATE 1**

There are about 270 species of marsupials. Most of them live in Australia*
and surrounding areas. Around 70 species live in the Americas. Gray
Kangaroos are about the size of a bee when they are born, but they can grow
up to 6 feet tall as adults. Baby kangaroos are called joeys.

**PLATE 2**

After it is born, a baby marsupial crawls through its mother's fur until it
reaches the pouch on her abdomen, where it attaches itself to a nipple
and drinks her milk. It keeps the nipple in its mouth until it has developed
enough to leave the pouch for short periods of time. The baby returns to
the pouch for nourishment, warmth, and safety until it is able to take care
of itself. Red-necked Wallaby babies spend about 8 months in the pouch,
but will continue to nurse until they are 12 to 17 months old. Adults stand
around 3 to 3 1/2 feet tall.

**PLATE 3**

Common Wombats (35 to 45 inches long**) are digging animals. They live
in burrows or holes that may be connected by tunnels up to 100 feet long.
The mother's rear-facing pouch keeps the dirt away from her baby when
she digs. Mother wombats are able to squeeze the muscles in their pouch
to keep the baby inside it.

* The marsupials illustrated are from Australia unless otherwise stated in the Afterword.
** Sizes vary. All measurements in the Afterword are approximate, and are for adult animals.

## PLATE 4

Not all marsupials have a fully developed pouch. Some have a loose flap of skin on their belly to protect the babies. Others, such as the Brown Antechinus (3 3/4 to 4 1/2 inches long, not including tail), do not have a pouch at all. The babies hang on to the mother's nipples until they get too heavy for her to carry around. Then she builds a nest and leaves them in it while she hunts for food.

## PLATE 5

Yellow-footed Rock Wallabies (20 to 30 inches long, not including tail) live in mountains and rocky places. They have rough pads on their feet that keep them from slipping as they leap from rock to rock. Rock wallabies are able to jump across gullies up to 13 feet wide.

Wooly Opossums (12 inches long, not including tail), one of the South American marsupials, can wrap their prehensile tails around branches to help them climb.

Sugar Gliders (5 to 7 inches long, not including tail) seem to "fly" from tree to tree. Their tails help with balance and steering. These marsupials jump from one tree, spread the flaps of skin on their sides, and glide to the next tree. They are called "Sugar" Gliders because they eat sweet foods such as tree sap, nectar, and fruit.

Eastern Quolls (24 to 31 inches long, including the tail) eat mostly insects, but they can run fast enough to catch small animals such as rabbits, mice, and ground-nesting birds. Eastern Quolls were also called "native cats" because they reminded the settlers of house cats.

**PLATE 6**
Grizzled Tree Kangaroos (2 1/2 to 3 feet tall) live in the rain forests in New Guinea. Tree kangaroos have strong arms and long claws to help them climb. They are able to leap from tree to tree. These marsupials eat mostly leaves and fruit. The fur on the shoulders of the Grizzled Tree Kangaroo grows in a reverse direction so that it will shed water like a raincoat.

**PLATE 7**
Greater Bilbies (12 to 24 inches long) live in deserts, grasslands, and dry scrub woodlands, where they dig burrows for sleeping. These marsupials are very rare partly because of rabbits that were introduced to Australia by European settlers. The rabbits multiplied rapidly, competing with the Greater Bilbies for food and destroying their habitat. Some Australians celebrate Easter with the "Easter Bilby" instead of the Easter Bunny. They hope that this kind of attention for one of their endangered marsupials will cause people to be more concerned with protecting native species.

**PLATE 8**
Marsupial Moles (3 to 8 inches long), like true moles, spend most of their time digging under the ground. They use their strong claws and the hard plate on their noses to push their way through loose, sandy soil. As they dig for worms and insects to eat, the tunnels they make cave in behind them. Like many other animals that live underground, Marsupial Moles are blind.

**PLATE 9**

Water Opossums or Yapoks (12 inches long, not including the tail) are the only marsupials that spend part of the time in water. They have water-repellent fur and webbed hind feet that help them swim well. To keep her babies from drowning while she hunts in the water, the mother shuts her pouch with a strong ring of muscle and makes it waterproof. Yapoks live in Central and South America.

**PLATE 10**

After hunting in the tropical forest all night, Cuscuses sleep sitting in trees during the day. They often wear the fur off their rumps by sitting so much. Cuscuses are slow-moving animals that climb well with their hand-shaped paws. Their strong, prehensile tails also help them hold on as they climb and sit. Only male Spotted Cuscuses (13 to 26 inches long, not including the tail) are spotted. The females usually have plain fur. These marsupials are found in New Guinea and surrounding areas as well as a small part of northeastern Australia.

**PLATE 11**

Numbats are diurnal. They find shelter in fallen logs in open woodlands during the night and look for food in the daytime. Their favorite foods are termites and ants that they dig out of rotten logs or anthills with strong sharp claws. They use their long sticky tongues to lap up the insects. Numbats (16 inches long, including the tail) can eat up to 20,000 termites a day.

### PLATE 12

Tasmanian Devils (20 to 30 inches long, not including the tail) are mostly scavengers, but will take live prey. Their powerful jaws and sharp teeth enable them to tear meat. Even though Devils mostly live alone, a group of them will often feed together on large carcasses. They jostle, snarl, and scream at each other as they try to eat their fill. Tasmanian Devils get their name from their fierce appearance and their bloodcurdling screams.

### PLATE 13

Koalas (2 to 3 feet long) eat the leaves from eucalyptus (gum) trees. Koalas get most of the water they need from leaves, but they will also drink if necessary. The word "koala" is thought to mean "no drink" in the native Aboriginal languages of Australia. Koalas are protected, but the forests where they live are not. These animals are in trouble because their homes and food sources are being destroyed.

### PLATE 14

Because Virginia Opossums (15 to 20 inches long, not including tail) will eat almost anything, they are able to live in many different habitats and are not in danger of extinction. They sometimes protect themselves by pretending to be dead—"playing possum." Virginia Opossums are the only marsupials that live in North America.

**PLATE 15**
Red Kangaroos are the largest marsupials. Adults can be over 6 feet tall and weigh up to 200 pounds. Red Kangaroos normally hop about 6 feet, but when in a hurry they can jump 30 feet. A group of kangaroos is called a "mob."

**PLATE 16**
Fat-tailed Dunnarts are 3 to 3 1/2 inches long, not including their tails, and weigh about 1 ounce. They eat insects and spiders. When there is plenty of food, Fat-tailed Dunnarts eat until their tails swell with fat. During times when food is hard to find, they are able to live off this stored fat. Their tails shrink as the fat is used up.

**PLATE 17**
Many marsupials are now on endangered, threatened, or vulnerable lists. Thylacines, sometimes called Tasmanian Wolves or Tasmanian Tigers, were neither wolves nor tigers. A fully grown Thylacine could be up to 6 feet long including the tail and 2 feet tall at the shoulder. Thylacines once ranged over most of Australia. Hunting, competition from introduced dogs, and habitat destruction caused the decline of Thylacines. This marsupial was officially declared extinct in 1986. Although there have been reports of Thylacine sightings, none have been confirmed since the last Thylacine died in captivity September 7, 1936.

# GLOSSARY

**Diurnal**—active during the day

**Extinct**—no longer existing in living form

**Mammal**—an animal that nourishes its young with milk secreted by mammary glands; most mammals have hair or fur on their skin

**Nocturnal**—active during the night

**Predator**—an animal that lives by hunting and feeding upon other animals

**Prehensile**—adapted for grasping

**Prey**—animals that are hunted and eaten by other animals

**Scavenger**—an animal that feeds on dead animals or decaying plants

**Species**—a group of closely related animals or plants

# BIBLIOGRAPHY

## BOOKS

Barrett, Norman. *Picture Library: Kangaroos and Other Marsupials*, New York: Franklin Watts, 1991.

Bender, Lionel. *First Sight: Kangaroos and Other Marsupials*, New York: Gloucester Press, 1988.

Books for World Explorers. *Amazing Animals of Australia*. Washington: National Geographic Society, 1985.

Burnie, David. *The Kingfisher Illustrated Animal Encyclopedia*. New York: Kingfisher, 2000.

Kalman, Bobbie, and Heather Levigne. *What is a Marsupial*? New York: Crabtree Publishing Company, 2000.

Swan, Erin Pembrey. *Meat-eating Marsupials*. New York: Franklin Watts, 2002.

## VIDEOS

*Really Wild Animals: Wonders Down Under*. National Geographic Kids Video. Washington: National Geographic Society, 1994.

## WEBSITES

*americazoo.com*
*animaldiversity.ummz.umich.edu*
*australian-animals.net*
*nationalgeographic.com/kids*

*sandiegozoo.net/animalbytes*
*wombania.com/wombats*
*42explore.com/marsupial.htm*

# ABOUT... SERIES

ISBN 978-1-56145-234-7 HC
ISBN 978-1-56145-312-2 PB

ISBN 978-1-56145-038-1 HC
ISBN 978-1-56145-364-1 PB

ISBN 978-1-56145-028-2 HC
ISBN 978-1-56145-147-0 PB

ISBN 978-1-56145-301-6 HC
ISBN 978-1-56145-405-1 PB

ISBN 978-1-56145-256-9 HC
ISBN 978-1-56145-335-1 PB

ISBN 978-1-56145-588-1 HC

ISBN 978-1-56145-207-1 HC
ISBN 978-1-66146-232-3 PB

ISBN 978-1-56145-141-8 HC
ISBN 978-1-56145-174-6 PB

ISBN 978-1-56145-358-0 HC
ISBN 978-1-56145-407-5 PB

ISBN 978-1-56145-331-3 HC
ISBN 978-1-56145-406-8 PB

ISBN 978-1-56145-488-4 HC
ISBN 978-1-56145-741-0 PB

ISBN 978-1-56145-454-9 HC

ISBN 978-1-56145-183-8 HC
ISBN 978-1-56145-233-0 PB

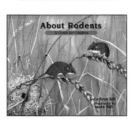

ISBN 978-1-56145-454-9 HC

# ABOUT HABITATS SERIES

ISBN 978-1-56145-390-0 HC
ISBN 978-1-56145-636-9 PB

ISBN 978-1-56145-559-1 HC

ISBN 978-1-56145-469-3 HC
ISBN 978-1-56145-731-1 PB

ISBN 978-1-56145-432-7 HC
ISBN 978-1-56145-689-5 PB

ISBN 978-1-56145-618-5 HC

ISBN 978-1-56145-734-2 HC

# THE SILLS

**Cathryn Sill**, a former elementary school teacher, is the author of the acclaimed ABOUT… and the ABOUT HABITATS series. With her husband John and brother-in-law Ben Sill, she coauthored three popular bird-guide parodies, including the new edition of A FIELD GUIDE TO LITTLE-KNOWN AND SELDOM-SEEN BIRDS OF NORTH AMERICA.

**John Sill** is a prize-winning and widely published wildlife artist who illustrates both the ABOUT… and the ABOUT HABITATS series. He also illustrated and coauthored the field guide parodies. A native of North Carolina, he holds a B.S. in wildlife biology from North Carolina State University.

The Sills live in North Carolina.